PERSPECTIVES ON HISTORY

CLEOPATRA

POWERFUL OR RUTHLESS LEADER PHARAOH?

by Peggy Caravantes

Raintree is an imprint of Capstone Global Library Limited, a company incorporated in England and Wales having its registered office at 7 Pilgrim Street, London, EC4V 6LB – Registered company number: 6695582

www.raintree.co.uk
myorders@raintree.co.uk

Editorial Credits
Brenda Haugen, editor; Heidi Thompson, designer; Svetlana Zhurkin, media researcher; Laura Manthe, production specialist

ISBN 978 1 406 29303 6 (hardback)
19 18 17 16 15
10 9 8 7 6 5 4 3 2 1

ISBN 978 1 406 29305 0 (paperback)
19 18 17 16 15
10 9 8 7 6 5 4 3 2 1

British Library Cataloguing in Publication Data
A full catalogue record for this book is available from the British Library.

Photo Credits
Alamy: classic/Roger Cracknell 01, 29, Mary Evans Picture Library, 7, Montagu Images, 23, North Wind Picture Archives, 13; Bridgeman Images: Look and Learn/Private Collection/The Death of Cleopatra, Nicolle, Pat (1907-95), 27, Look and Learn/Private Collection/When They Were Young: Cleopatra's Childhood, Jackson, Peter (1922-2003), 5, 9; Getty Images: DeAgostini, 19; iStockphotos: hrstklnkr, 15; Newscom: akg-images, 16, 25, akg-images/Werner Forman, 6, Album/Oronoz, 21; Shutterstock: Galyna Andrushko, cover (background); SuperStock: Christie's Images Ltd., cover (bottom), DeAgostini, cover (middle right), Fine Art Images, 12, Tips Images, 11; XNR Productions, 17

Design Elements by Shutterstock

Every effort has been made to contact [...] [omi]ssions will be rectified in subsequent printing[...]

All the Internet addresses (URLs) give[...] [...]er, due to the dynamic nature of the Internet, so[...] [...]r ceased to exist since publication. While the au[...] [...]eaders, no responsibility for any such changes [...]

Printed and bound in China

CONTENTS

An unusual introduction

A small, two-oared boat glided quietly into the harbour at Alexandria, Egypt, and docked. The oarsman, a big man called Apollodorus, picked up a large **hemp** bag tied with a leather cord. Then he set off towards the Egyptian palace.

Apollodorus moved swiftly and silently, looking from side to side. Soon he arrived at the private quarters of Julius Caesar. Apollodorus entered and laid the bag on the floor in front of the Roman ruler. Apollodorus untied the cord, and a young woman crawled out of the bag and stood before Caesar. She was Cleopatra VII, the **exiled** queen of Egypt.

Cleopatra had been driven out of Alexandria by her brother's advisers. She was determined to get her throne back. But there was danger in Egypt. Her brother's soldiers were everywhere. They had instructions to kill Cleopatra if she tried to get back into the palace.

The strong-willed Cleopatra did not give up. She and Apollodorus came up with the plan to sneak into the palace where Caesar was staying. Cleopatra would seek Caesar's help to overthrow her brother Ptolemy XIII.

hemp plant that produces fibre

exile order to leave one's country; or to leave voluntarily

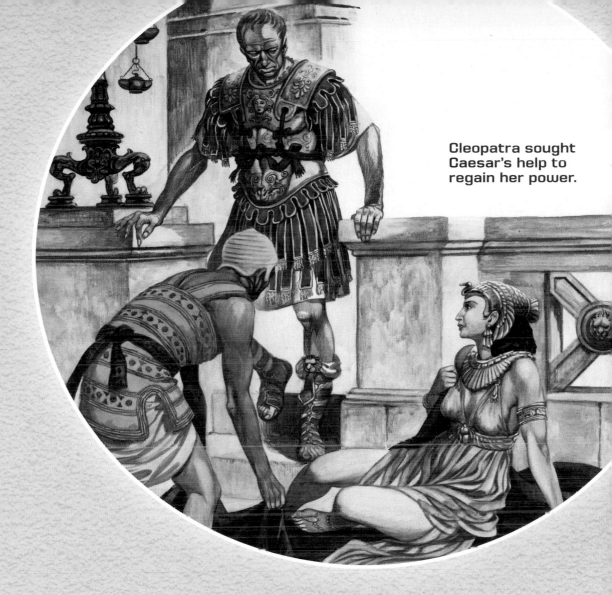

Cleopatra sought Caesar's help to regain her power.

If Caesar rejected her plea for help, she would be in great danger. But no risk was too great to regain her throne. It belonged to her. She was Egypt's **pharaoh**, and she would do anything to regain her power. She needed Rome's power and money to help her. The only way to get it was to meet Julius Caesar face-to-face.

pharaoh king or queen of ancient Egypt

Chapter 1

A FEMALE RULER IN A MAN'S WORLD

Cleopatra VII is one of the most famous women from ancient times. She belonged to a royal family from Macedonia, Greece. Her family had begun ruling Egypt after the death of Alexander the Great of Macedonia. All the main rulers of this line of Greek kings of Egypt were named Ptolemy. They were also all male, except for the last one: Cleopatra VII.

NOT A FAMOUS FACE

Though Cleopatra VII is famous, no one really knows what she looked like. The only images of her, from the time, are those found on Egyptian coins. They show a woman with strong, bold features and her hair tied back into a bun. Coin makers may have made her look more like a man in order to compete with male rivals.

Ptolemy I (centre) was the first of Cleopatra's ancestors to rule Egypt.

In the 300 years that the Ptolemies ruled, Cleopatra was the only pharaoh who spoke Egyptian. She and her four brothers and sisters received a broad education. Historians believe Cleopatra may have learned to speak as many as nine languages.

Cleopatra's father, Ptolemy XII, died in 51 BC. Cleopatra and her younger brother Ptolemy XIII became Egypt's rulers. She was 18 years old, and he was 10 years old. For a while the two lived in their palace at Alexandria: Egypt's capital and the world's largest city at the time. In Egypt the male usually ruled, so three advisers helped the younger ruler to make decisions. Through him they hoped to control Egypt. They gained complete control over the young king as they conspired against Cleopatra.

For three years, the strong-willed and ambitious Cleopatra took on most of the ruling duties. She was still the ruler despite the efforts of her brother's advisers to gain control of the country. Cleopatra had the approval and respect of the Egyptian people. She hoped to bring Egypt back to its former size and glory. She wanted to recover lands lost in battle. But the Roman republic surrounded Egypt on all sides. Cleopatra had to protect her people from Rome's attempts to conquer Egypt. However, Ptolemy XIII's advisers wanted to rule through the young boy. They used his army to force Cleopatra into exile in Syria when she was 20 years old.

Cleopatra was determined to get her power back.
She started to raise an army to fight against her brother.
Before she could act, Julius Caesar arrived in Alexandria.

Queen Cleopatra ruled alongside her brother.

Chapter 2

MEETING JULIUS CAESAR

Julius Caesar and a rival leader, Pompey, were fighting in a **civil war** because both wanted to rule the Roman Empire. When Pompey's forces began losing, he fled to Egypt. He expected protection from Ptolemy XIII. Pompey had promised to help the now 14-year-old ruler hold on to the Egyptian throne. But Ptolemy XIII did not want to anger Caesar by helping Pompey. When Pompey arrived in Egypt, Ptolemy XIII ordered his murder.

Although they had battled for power, Caesar and Pompey were both Romans and relatives. Caesar was upset that Egyptians had murdered his daughter's husband. He went to Egypt to find out who had killed Pompey. He also planned to urge Cleopatra and her brother to work together, because a stable Egypt was good for Rome. Caesar moved into the Egyptian palace at Alexandria.

civil war war between different sections or parties of the same country or nation

Julius Caesar turned the Roman republic into the powerful Roman Empire.

From her exile in Syria, Cleopatra heard about Caesar's arrival in Egypt. She decided to seek his help in regaining her throne. She travelled to Egypt by boat to avoid meeting any of her brother's soldiers. Under cover of darkness, she and her servant Apollodorus slipped into the harbour at Alexandria.

In Caesar's quarters young Cleopatra VII stood before the 52-year-old Roman ruler. Cleopatra flattered and charmed him, but her sharp mind and clear speech attracted Caesar even more. As they talked they began to fall in love and decided to help each other. With Caesar's armies aiding her, Cleopatra could defeat her brother's army and take back the Egyptian throne. With her riches she could help Caesar ease Rome's debt. For six months the two sides fought on land and on sea. Finally, Ptolemy's army gave up. Cleopatra was crowned queen of Egypt again. She shared the throne with her other brother, Ptolemy XIV, but in name only. Ptolemy XIV had the title of king, but Cleopatra had all the power.

Cleopatra and Caesar were both strong rulers.

While Cleopatra and Caesar lived together in Alexandria, Caesar learned that Cleopatra's younger brother had ordered Pompey's murder. He sent soldiers after Ptolemy XIII. While trying to escape, the young ruler drowned in the River Nile.

After her brother's death, Cleopatra wanted to show off her riches and her support for Rome. She sailed with Caesar on the royal barge along the same river where her brother had died. All along the way, the people cheered her. Caesar saw all that Egypt offered. He hoped to marry Cleopatra and to join the two nations. With their combined power and wealth, Caesar believed he could become like a god. Cleopatra shared the dream. She would be not only a ruler, but also a goddess of Egypt.

FACT
Cleopatra wore jewelled sandals with patterns on the soles to show off her wealth.

Cleopatra sailed the River Nile on her royal barge.

With Cleopatra back in power, Caesar returned to Rome. He did not know that Cleopatra was pregnant. In 47 BC she gave birth to a son she called Caesarion, or "little Caesar". However, Caesar never claimed the child as his son.

The next year Cleopatra joined Caesar in Rome. She hoped to convince him to make Caesarion his **heir**. By this time Caesar had defeated many of his rivals.

However, several members of the Roman Senate envied and feared Caesar's power. They also feared his relationship with Cleopatra. Rumours had spread that Caesar planned to make himself king, and Cleopatra queen, and that they would move the capital of Rome to Alexandria. Rather than risk that happening, they killed Caesar on 15 March 44 BC.

Cleopatra feared she might be killed as well. She returned to Egypt with thoughts of killing her brother. He was now 15 years old and demanding equal power with Cleopatra. According to law, no queen could rule alone. The only person Cleopatra wanted to share the throne with was her son, Caesarion. Not long after Cleopatra's return, Ptolemy XIV mysteriously died from poisoning. Historians believe that either Cleopatra or one of her servants killed him. Young Caesarion took his place at Cleopatra's side, and together they now ruled Egypt.

FACT
Cleopatra believed she was the Egyptian goddess Isis reborn.

heir someone who has been or will be left a title, property or money

14

Caesar's murder, as painted by the German artist Karl Theodor Piloty

Chapter 3

ANTONY AND CLEOPATRA

After Caesar's death, three men ruled the Roman Empire together. They were Mark Antony, Lepidus and Octavian, Caesar's adopted son and heir. Their first goal was to **avenge** Caesar's death. Cleopatra was concerned about this new leadership. She feared they would not support her as Egypt's queen. To gain their favour, she decided to help them. She brought a fleet of ships to Greece to join their armies at Philippi.

During the journey a big storm damaged her ships. Cleopatra became terribly seasick. She returned to Alexandria and prepared to sail again to the conflict. But before she could get the ships ready, Caesar's enemies were defeated at Philippi.

Mark Antony, Octavian and Lepidus had to work together as equal leaders.

After the battle, Antony and Octavian divided their powers. Antony established himself in the east and began travelling through the territory. He arrived in the Roman city of Tarsus in 41 BC. From there he ordered Cleopatra to meet him. Antony did not know she planned to help him avenge Caesar's death. Instead he thought she had helped the **assassins** to kill Caesar. Cleopatra wanted to talk to Antony about joining forces for the benefit of both countries. She did not like taking orders, though, and ignored Antony's demands to meet. She would meet on her own terms.

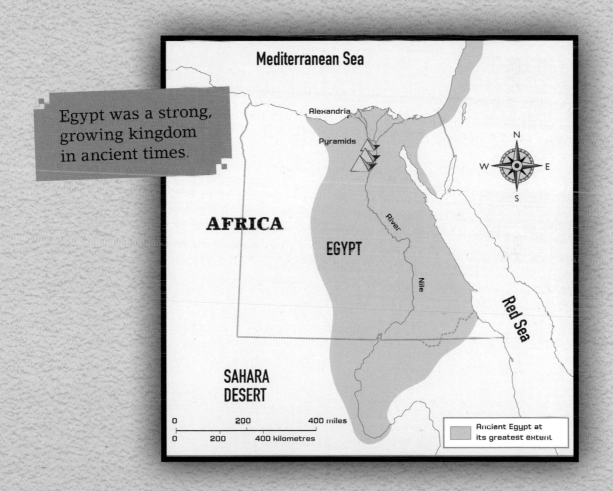

Egypt was a strong, growing kingdom in ancient times.

avenge take revenge for

assassin person who kills an important person, such as a king or queen

When she finally went to join the new Roman leader in Tarsus, Cleopatra went as a powerful queen. She decorated her ships and chose beautiful clothes to wear at their meeting. She impressed Antony. He was happy to learn Cleopatra was not involved in Caesar's death.

Soon Cleopatra and Antony fell in love. They agreed that Octavian should not be Caesar's heir and the ruler of Rome. Their reasoning for this was different. Cleopatra wanted the title for her son, Caesarion. Antony wanted the title for himself. They continued to make plans, and Antony followed Cleopatra back to Egypt.

Antony returned to his duties in Rome in the spring of 40 BC. He and Cleopatra did not see each other again for over three years. Not long after he left, Cleopatra gave birth to twins: Alexander Helios and Cleopatra Selene. For a few years after the twins' births, little is known about Cleopatra's actions. However, as queen, she kept an eye on politics in Rome.

Antony and Octavian had pledged to work together. Part of their agreement was for Antony to marry Octavian's sister Octavia. This union made Cleopatra uneasy. She wanted to protect her position with Antony. She met Antony in Rome in 37 BC. A special ceremony was planned at that time for the three leaders: Antony, Octavian and Lepidus. During the ceremony, the Roman Senate appointed the three men to lead the Empire for another five years.

Cleopatra (centre, in blue) landed at Tarsus to meet with Antony.

THE ROYAL KITCHEN

Cleopatra's court was famous for its lavish meals. Food had to be ready at all times. One day, the cooks were roasting 8 boars for only 12 guests. Each wild boar was at a different stage of being ready to eat. This meant that when Cleopatra demanded they be served, the meat of one of the boars was just right. The other boars were thrown away.

After the ceremony, the men decided Antony should lead an attack on Parthia to expand the Roman Empire. But Antony needed more money for this venture. He invited Cleopatra to meet him at Antioch. This time she did not hesitate to meet him. She saw this as an opportunity to make the bond between Rome and Egypt even stronger. She believed that together they would one day rule the world. She wanted to take part in the planning.

In the spring of 36 BC, Antony set out to take over Parthia. As he marched eastwards, Antony gave the conquered lands to Cleopatra in exchange for the money she gave him for the expedition. Egyptians did not seem to worry about the relationship between their queen and Antony. They were pleased that Antony was giving the conquered land to Egypt. This helped fulfill Cleopatra's goal of making Egypt powerful again. While Antony was gone, Cleopatra gave birth to their third child, Ptolemy Philadelphus.

The battle in Parthia did not go well for Antony. He lost men instead of gaining land. By late autumn he gave up and sent a message to Cleopatra. He asked her to meet him at the coast and to send clothes for his soldiers and money. Historians disagree about whether Cleopatra went to Antony as soon as she could. Some believe she waited to consider the situation. Others say that she needed time to gather enough money. It was several weeks before she arrived. By then the soldiers were in rags, and Antony was desperate.

Antony wanted to rule the Roman Empire alone.

After his defeat in Parthia in late 36 BC, Antony went back to Egypt with Cleopatra. He wanted to stay away from Rome because he had sent Octavian false reports of victories in Parthia. While Antony hid in Egypt, Cleopatra made sure of her own strength as a ruler. She had spent the winter making alliances with her neighbouring nations to strengthen her position as a leader. Among them was an agreement with the king of Media to combine forces against the Parthians.

The agreement allowed Antony to again set out for Parthia. Along the way he had trouble with the king of Armenia. After capturing the king and his family, Antony turned back to Alexandria. In Egypt he paraded the royal family, bound in gold chains, as spoils of war. Romans were upset that the **triumph** was celebrated in Egypt instead of Rome. Romans believed Cleopatra controlled Antony's actions. They resented her power over him.

Octavian decided to build on his countrymen's anger against his fellow ruler. He found a document, which he said was Antony's will. The will revealed that Antony wanted to be buried in Alexandria. Octavian's followers used Antony's desire to be buried in Alexandria as evidence that he wanted to move Rome's capital there. This further angered Roman citizens.

triumph great success or victory

Cleopatra and Antony in Egypt

Chapter 4

FINAL BATTLE

Romans knew war was coming. Octavian was planning to get rid of his rival, Antony. Hearing this news, Antony and Cleopatra fled to Greece. There they prepared their own naval forces to meet those of Octavian. Other ships and troops joined them. The two sides clashed on the Ionian Sea near Actium in 31 BC. When the battle turned against them, Cleopatra wanted to save her fleet and retreated with her ships. Antony's forces were too small to stand up to Octavian, and Antony was forced to surrender.

Cleopatra no longer believed Antony could protect Egypt from a Roman takeover. Cleopatra could lose everything — her land, her power, her wealth. She sent a message to Antony stating that she was dead. She hoped the news of her death would cause him to kill himself. Antony's death would provide Cleopatra with more options when dealing with Octavian. Even if she wasn't queen, she still had power. She was the mother of Caesar's child, and the mother of three of Antony's children. These reasons alone might encourage Octavian to let Cleopatra live.

Cleopatra's message to Antony worked. Unable to live without her, Antony fell on his sword, but he did not die. His assistants carried Antony's bleeding body to Cleopatra. Antony was shocked that she still lived, but he urged her to make peace with Octavian. Then Antony died in Cleopatra's arms.

Cleopatra feared Octavian would now conquer Egypt. Despite her importance, Cleopatra was terrified that Octavian might take her and her children in chains to Rome to parade as spoils of war. Unable to face such an embarrassment, she killed herself. Legend says she had a poisonous snake brought to her in a basket of figs. She put the snake on her chest and allowed it to bite her. More recent research suggests she drank a mixture of poisons.

Whatever means she used, Cleopatra died at the age of 39, and she and Antony were buried together. The Ptolemy family's 300-year **dynasty** ended after Cleopatra had ruled for about 22 years.

FACT
After Cleopatra's death, Egypt became a Roman province.

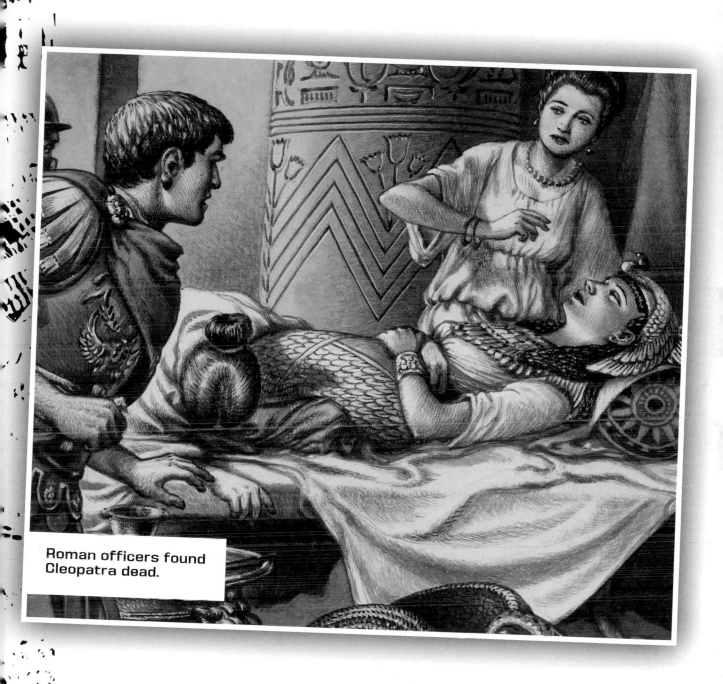

Roman officers found
Cleopatra dead.

dynasty period of time during which a country's rulers all come from one family

Chapter 5

CLEOPATRA'S LEGACY

Although most of Egypt's queens have been forgotten, the memory of Cleopatra lives on. Men who had never met Cleopatra wrote her life story. They pictured her as a beautiful **siren** who tempted and destroyed men. They focused on Cleopatra's ties to Julius Caesar and Mark Antony. Early writers claimed she used the two men to reach her own goals. They also wrote about Cleopatra killing her **siblings** in her climb to power.

FACT
After Cleopatra's death, Antony's and her three children were brought up by Octavia.

siren tempting woman
sibling brother or sister

A bronze statue of Cleopatra in Alexandria, Egypt

However, from about AD 640, writers started looking differently at Cleopatra's role in Egypt's history. She had successfully ruled in a man's world. She restored lands lost by male rulers. She saved Egypt from being overtaken by the Roman Empire. One of her names was Cleopatra Philopatris, which means "she who loves her country". Some historians believe that if Cleopatra had not killed herself, she might have ruled even more of the world.

So who was Cleopatra — a powerful leader or a ruthless pharaoh? What do you think?

GLOSSARY

assassin person who kills an important person, such as a king or queen

avenge take revenge for

civil war war between different sections or parties of the same country or nation

dynasty period of time during which a country's rulers all come from one family

exile order to leave one's country; or to leave voluntarily

heir someone who has been or will be left a title, property or money

hemp plant that produces fibre

pharaoh king or queen of ancient Egypt

sibling brother or sister

siren tempting woman

triumph great success or victory

READ MORE

Ancient Egypt (Eyewitness), Dorling Kindersley (Dorling Kindersley, 2014)

Cleopatra (Great Women Leaders), Jane Bingham (Raintree, 2009)

Julius Caesar (Hero Journals), Nick Hunter (Raintree, 2014)

What did the ancient Egyptians do for me? (Linking the Past and Present), Patrick Catel (Raintree, 2011)

WEBSITES

www.bbc.co.uk/history/historic_figures/cleopatra.shtml

Find out more about Cleopatra's life history.

www.bbc.co.uk/history/forkids/

Follow the links to take on the Pyramid Challenge and to complete the construction of the pharaoh's tomb.

www.ngkids.co.uk/did-you-know/Ten-Facts-about-Ancient-Egypt

Ten fascinating facts about Ancient Egypt!

COMPREHENSION QUESTIONS

1. Cleopatra gave her twins interesting second names. She gave her son Helios, meaning "sun", and her daughter Selene, meaning "moon". Why do you think she chose these second names?

2. If you were writing a story about Cleopatra, what information would you include about her brothers? Refer to details in the text.

3. Cleopatra decided to leave Actium with her fleet of ships. Was it a good or bad decision? Support your answer with details from the text.

INDEX